Lyrical
Life Science
Workbook

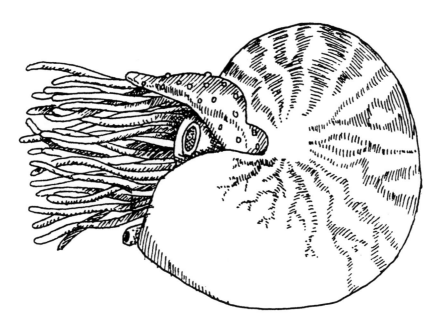

By
Doug and Dorry Eldon

Illustrations
by
Eric Altendorf

How to use this workbook:

The emphasis of this Lyrical Learning project is to help the student learn the anguage of life science in an enjoyable way through the avenue of song. The worksheets expand on the information from the songs and may be used to reinforce the information. They may be used for review and learning in which the student refers back to the textbook for the needed information, or they may be used as tests. Answers are given in the answer key at the back of the book, including essay answers. (The student's answers need not be worded the same.) You may wish to remove the answer key before the student begins the workbook.

Each song and chapter of the accompanying textbook and CD or MP3 are given three worksheets in this workbook. The pages within a given select section are progressive in that they require deeper levels of understanding.

The first page for each chapter is a fill-in-the blank lyric sheet to simply reinforce information learned by the song. The student should know the song before attempting the worksheet.

The second page of each chapter contains questions which are objective: true/false, matching, fill-in=the-blank and short answer–which use information from the song and textbook. These pages require more understanding of the subject matter.

The third page of each chapter contains essay questions which often require a further synthesis and application of the information from the textbook and song. Many of the questions require a greater understanding than the recalling of facts on the objective worksheets.

Even more thought-provoking questions are asked on the third page under the heading DIGGING DEEPER. These questions require further research. The sutdent may not be ready to answer these questions, but it would be worthwhile to read the answers supplied to broaden the student's understanding and promote discussion.

Cover design: Susan Moore
Illustrations: Eric Altendorf
Copyright: Douglas Eldon 1995
Reproducible for individual classroom use.

Lyrical Learning

Lyrical Learning
8008 Cardwell Hill
Corvallis, Oregon 97330
Telephone 541-754-3579

TABLE OF CONTENTS

THE SCIENTIFIC METHOD - Lyrics

Oh, what do you think a_____ does
To solve a _____ found because
Many _____ are scientists
'Cause they're great_____ solvers
There is a_____ way

They go about 'most every day
It's _____ and it's _____
The _____ method

Chorus: A way to_____ a problem, a way, a way
The_____ _____ is a way to solve a _____
  A way, a way, a way to _____ a problem
  A way, a way, a way to solve a _____

It may not seem important to you
But the _____ thing that they always do
Is state the _____ or ask a _____
So they know just what they're after
Then they _____ everything involved
That might help get the _____ solved
By reading, _____
And gathering _____
Chorus

After both of these _____ they take
They go ahead and then they make
An educated guess—a _____—
A possible _____
Then they use _____ tools
To _____ and test some variables
In _____ which are really meant
To give more _____
Chorus

This information they call _____
They put together so that later
They can analyze and _____
To see just what it all means
Only when they have done all these
_____ testing _____
Which may prove, or else _____
Then they'll state their _____
Chorus

This is the _____ way
A _____ may use any old day
'Cause it's _____ and it's logical
The _____ _____

Fill in the blanks, you may use words more than once.

conclusion
data
disprove
experiments
first
hypotheses
hypothesis
information
logical
measure
method
methodical
problem
question
researching
review
scientific
scientist
scientists
solution
solve
steps
synthesize
systematic

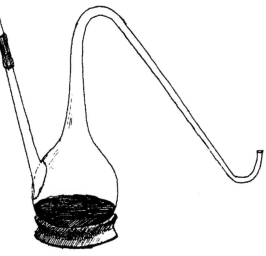

THE SCIENTIFIC METHOD - Objective

True or false

1 - _____ Pasteur proved that germs are carried in the air.

2 - _____ Microbes can be easily seen.

3 - _____ A variable does not change the outcome of an experiment.

4 - _____ Microscopes were first used in the early 1900's.

5 - _____ A hypothesis is a possible answer to a problem.

Matching

6 - Pasteur _____   A. Following orderly steps

7 - methodical _____   B. Discovered that microbes were killed by boiling

8 - variables _____   C. An educated guess, a possible solution

9 - Spallanzani _____   D. Factors that may affect the result of an experiment

10 - hypothesis _____   E. Proved microbes were carried on dust in the air

List the six steps of the scientific method in proper order:

11 - _____ Analyze data

12 - _____ Gather information

13 - _____ State a conclusion

14 - _____ Ask a question or state the problem

15 - _____ Experiment

16 - _____ Make a hypothesis

Fill in the blank

17 - A hypothesis can be tested by conducting _____.

18 - A hypothesis is an educated guess or a _____ _____.

19 - The information collected during experiments is often called _____.

20 - A _____ is stated after data is analyzed.

THE SCIENTIFIC METHOD - Essay

1 - Compare step one of the scientific method (ask a question or state the problem) with solving a math story problem. _____

_____

_____

_____

_____

2 - Why is it important to gather information by reviewing, reading and researching?

_____

_____

_____

3 - Why is it important to control variables in an experiment? _____

_____

_____

_____

4 - Why is it important to follow the steps of the scientific method in order?

_____

_____

_____

_____

5 - What can be done with data to make it easier to analyze? _____

_____

DIGGING DEEPER

1 - Scientists might not be able to prove that their hypothesis was correct. Why is it important for scientists to be willing to admit that their educated guess was wrong, even after all the work they did?_____

_____

_____

_____

_____

2 - If a hypothesis is a possible explanation or solution, what is a theory and what is a law?

THEORY:_____

_____

LAW: _____

_____

4

ALL LIVING THINGS - Lyrics

All living things are able to _____
Move and _____ and respond to a _____
And carry on _____ activities
These are _____ of living things

There are four metabolic _____:
Ingestion and _____ are two of these
_____and excretion
Metabolic, metabolic: _____ activities

Needs of living things include_____
Water, _____ and food to eat
Living space and proper _____
All living things have these _____ basic needs

Living things are all made up of _____
Units of _____ and functions you can tell
All _____ come only from other living _____.
This is what's called the _____ theory

_____ that are similar joined together form _____
_____ working together form _____
Organ _____ and _____ are:
Five levels in which living things are _____

Kingdom , _____, class, _____ , _____
Genus and _____ make the _____ you see
_____ and taxonomy
Classify, classify, name and classify

ALL LIVING THINGS - Objective

Match the letter of the kingdom at the top with the characteristics below.

   A. Monera   B. Protozoa   C. Fungi   D. Plant   E. Animal

1- ____ - cell wall   2 - ____ - no cell wall   3 - ____ - no cell wall
- nucleus   - nucleus   - nucleus
- no chlorophyll   - no chlorophyll   - no chlorophyll
- absorbs food   - many-celled   - single-cell organism
                       - ingests food   - makes, absorbs, or
                                           ingests food

4 - ____ - cell wall   5 - ____ - cell wall
- nucleus   - no nucleus
- chlorophyll
- makes food

Number the five levels of organization in living things from the simplest to most complex:

  6 - Tissues   _____
  7 - Single cell   _____
  8 - Organism   _____
  9 - Organs   _____
10 - Organ systems _____

Number the seven levels of classification; the most general to the most specific:

11 - Phylum   _____
12 - Order   _____
13 - Kingdom   _____
14 - Family   _____
15 - Species   _____
16 - Genus   _____
17 - Class   _____

What are the two parts to scientific names?

18 - _____   19 - _____

List the six basic needs of living things.

20 - _____
21 - _____
22 - _____
23 - _____
24 - _____
25 - _____

ALL LIVING THINGS - Essay/Short Answer

1 - What are the three main points of the cell theory?

    1._____

    2._____

    3._____

A food chain is a simple way to describe how energy is transferred or passed, from one organism to another. Describe and give examples of the four places in a food chain:

2 - PRODUCER: _____

    example: _____

3 - PRIMARY CONSUMER: _____

    example: _____

4 - SECONDARY CONSUMER: _____

    example: _____

5 - DECOMPOSER: _____

    example: _____

Identify which cell is an animal cell and which is a plant cell:

6 - _____   7 - _____

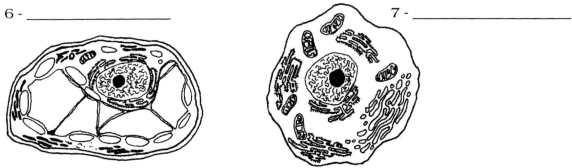

8 - What are two main differences between the plant and the animal cell?

    1._____

    2._____

DIGGING DEEPER

1 - Use a classification system to describe where you live, beginning with the most general and ending with the most specific:

    1 - <u>Continent</u>   Street name

    2 - _____   City

    3 - _____   State

    4 - _____   Country

    5 - _____   Street number

    6 - _____   Continent

    7 - _____   County

2 - How are scientific names more accurate than common names?

_____

_____

INVERTEBRATES - Lyrics

Many _____ have different features
   yet all have a common _____:
With no backbone they are all known
   to be called _____

All invertebrates together make a bit
  over ___ percent
Of the animal species in the world
  they live in any _____

They're divided into _____ ,
  by their _____ classified
Here are eight kinds if you do find
  Can then be identified

_____ are really sponges
  and they all have tiny _____
Cells in colonies they surely are pleased
  living on the ocean floor

Cnidarians like jellyfish, corals
  hydra, sea anemone
Cells for _____ have one opening
  _____body cavity

Platyhelminths are the _____
  like the small planarians
Nematodes are little _____
  segmented worms are _____

Echinoderms have _____ skins and
  tube feet coming out of them
Sea cucumber, _____ , sand dollar
  and the spiny sea urchin

Slugs and snails are one-shelled _____
  clams and scallops have _____ shells
Octopus, squid, nautilus are
  headfooted with _____

They all have a softish body
  with a _____ that can make
A hard shell that you can tell will
  give _____ for their sake

Arthropods have jointed legs
  and a hard _____
Centipedes, millipedes, insects
  arachnids, crustaceans

Centipedes have fewer legs and
  they are also _____
Millipedes have many more legs
  _____ and herbivores

Crabs and lobsters, _____ and barnacles
  are _____ you can tell
Four _____ , legs are many
  they're aquatic with a shell

Arachnids include the spiders
  ticks and mites and _____
They all have _____legs two body parts
  No antennae and no wings

Insects have ____ legs, three body parts
  _____ antennae and two eyes
Egg to _____ change to _____
  then to _____ with wings to fly

Fill in the blanks, you may use words more than once.

adults	crustaceans	habitat	mollusks	pupa	six	structures
annelids	eight	hollow	phyla	roundworms	spiders	tenacles
antennae	eighty-nine	invertebrate	pores	scavengers	spiny	trait
carnivores	exoskeleton	larva	Poriferans	scorpions	starfish	tube
creatures	flatworms	mantle	protection	shrimp	stinging	two

INVERTEBRATES - Objective

Match the phylum on the left with the characteristics and examples on the right.

A. Poriferans

1 - ____ spiny skin, suction-tipped tube feet

B. Cnidarians

2 - ____ jointed legs, exoskeleton

C. Platyhelminths

3 - ____ tiny pores, cells live in colonies

D. Nematodes

4 - ____ soft body, mantle that can make a hard shell

E. Annelids

5 - ____ hollow body cavity, one opening, stinging cells

F. Echinoderms

6 - ____ worm with a flat body, no segments

G. Mollusks

7 - ____ worm with a round, threadlike body, no segments

H. Arthropods

8 - ____ worm with segmented body

Examples:

9 - ____ insects, arachnids, crustaceans, centipedes, millipedes

10 - ____ coral, jellyfish, hydra, sea anemone

11 - ____ sea urchin, sea star, sea cucumber, sand dollar, sea lily

12 - ____ squid, slug, snail, octopus, nautilus, bivalves

Match the name of the class of arthropods on the left with characteristics and examples on the right.

A. Insects

13 - ____ aquatic; gills; 4 antennae; many body segments; many legs (10 or more); often have claws or pinchers

B. Arachnids

14 - ____ 6 legs; 3 body segments; 2 antennae; 0, 2 or 4 wings, usually 2 compound eyes

C. Crustaceans

15 - ____ 8 legs; 2 body segments; no antennae; no wings; 0 to many simple eyes; some have pinchers

D. Millipedes

16 - ____ many legs (50 or more); 4 legs per body segment; body that can curl up; herbivores/scavengers

E. Centipedes

17 - ____ many legs (30 or more); 2 legs per body segment; somewhat flat body that wiggles like a snake; carnivores

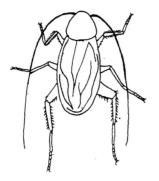

Examples:

18 - ____ lobsters, crabs, barnacles, shrimp, prawns, crayfish

'19 - ____ spiders, scorpions, ticks, mites, horseshoe crabs

20 - ____ flies, beetles, wasps, grasshoppers, butterflies, termites

INVERTEBRATES - Essay/Short Answer

1 - List the phyla of invertebrates and the one class or arthropods which are mainly aquatic. _____
_____
_____

2 - Describe the stages of complete metamorphosis of a moth. _____
_____
_____
_____

3 - How are invertebrates classified? _____
_____

4 - How do poriferans obtain their food?_____
_____

5 - Listed are several kinds of mollusks available in grocery stores. Identify them as:

   G - gastropods   ____ Scallops
     (univalves)   ____ Mussel
   P - pelecypods   ____ Squid
     (bivalves)   ____ Escargot (snail)
   C - cephalopods   ____ Octopus
     (head-footed mollusks) ____ Oyster
                        ____ Clam

6 - What characteristics can be used to identify different classes of arthropods?
_____
_____

7 - The ability to fly gives insects what advantages over other invertebrates?
_____
_____

DIGGING DEEPER

1 - Why have insects been so successful in inhabiting the earth? _____
_____
_____
_____

2 - Research and list the common names or give examples for these other phyla of invertebrates:

Ctenophora -_____   Echiura - _____
Nemertina -_____   Tardigrada - _____
Rotifera - _____   Penastoma - _____
Nematomorpha -_____   Onychophora - _____
Ectoprocta - _____   Pogonophora - _____
Brachiopoda -_____   Chaetognatha - _____
Sipuncula -_____   Hemichordata - _____

COLDBLOODED VERTEBRATES - Lyrics

Oh, when you study animals, there're some of which you're told

Whose _____ will always stay quite warm; but some whose blood is _____

They can _____ within a range

Of temperature except a change

That's too _____ can be so dangerous for animals

For coldblooded _____ ; coldblooded animals

They must respond by what they do and so they move around

To find the proper _____ in water or on ground

Fish, _____ , _____ ,

Whose temperature of blood has been

Controlled from _____ not within these kinds of animals

These coldblooded vertebrates; coldblooded animals

The fish have _____ instead of _____ to get their oxygen

And most have air _____ and _____ to help them float and _____

Some are jawless, like _____

With _____ like sharks and rays

But most have bony _____ , they're bony animals

They're coldblooded _____ ; coldblooded animals

Amphibians lead double lives, that's how they get their name

They start in water, then go on _____ , which they like just the same

_____ have dry and bumpy skin

_____ is wet and smooth as in

The salamanders and _____ , their kin. They're all _____

They're coldblooded vertebrates; coldblooded animals

Snakes and lizards are _____ , along with _____

Whose legs are made for _____ , not for swimming like _____

Crocodiles have teeth that _____

An _____ will always go

Inside its _____ that's how to know these different animals

These coldblooded vertebrates; coldblooded animals

These animals are different in the way they reproduce

The fish must _____ their eggs _____ and loose

Amphibians' _____ _____ are wet

Reptiles' are _____ and set

To hatch on _____ where they will get to become animals

These coldblooded animals; coldblooded animals

Fill in the blanks, you may use words more than once.
alligator's
amphibians
animals
bladders
blood
cartilage
cold
externally
extreme
fertilize
fins
frog's
gills
jelly eggs
lampreys
land
leathery
lungs
mouth
newts
outside
reptiles
show
survive
swim
swimming
temperature
toads
tortoises
turtles
vertebrae
vertebrates
walking
warm

COLDBLOODED VERTEBRATES - Objective

True or false

1 - _____ Reptiles lay jelly-like eggs.

2 - _____ Salamanders keep their tails as adults.

3 - _____ Fish have gills, fins, scales and backbones.

4 - _____ Amphibians have dry and scaly skin.

5 - _____ Amphibians can live in water and on land.

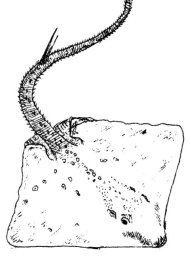

Matching

6 - Cobra _____   A. Jawless fish

7 - Bullfrog _____   B. Cartilaginous fish

8 - Lamprey _____   C. Bony Fish

9 - Perch _____   D. Amphibian

10 - Manta ray _____   E. Reptile

Fill in the blank

11 - Young amphibians live in _____ , feed on _____ _____ , breathe
    through _____ , and have a _____ that gradually disappears.

12 - Reptiles have skin that is _____ and _____.

13 - Fins help fish to _____ , _____ and _____.

14 - Bony fish are different from jawless fish in that they have _____ ,
    and _____ , and most also have air _____.

15 - Fish, reptiles, and amphibians are similar in that they all are _____
    and have a _____.

Short answer

16 - What is the main difference between an adult toad and an adult frog? _____

_____

17 - How do fish fertilize their eggs? _____

_____

18 - What are two differences between amphibians and reptiles?_____

_____

_____

19 - Why is it important to wet your hands before handling frogs, salamanders
    or newts?_____

_____

_____

20 - List three differing characteristics for tadpoles and adult frogs.

    Tadpole _____   Adult frog _____

            _____   _____

            _____   _____

COLDBLOODED VERTEBRATES - Essay

1 - How does a coldblooded vertebrate keep its body temperature constant? Give an example._____

_____

_____

_____

2 - Describe an amphibian life cycle. _____

_____

_____

_____

_____

3 - Describe characteristics used to distinguish:

jawless fish: _____

_____

cartilaginous fish: _____

_____

bony fish:_____

_____

4 - Compare and contrast the reproduction of fish, reptiles and amphibians.

_____

_____

_____

_____

_____

DIGGING DEEPER

Why would you not find a snake crawling on the snow in Alaska in the winter?

_____

_____

_____

_____

_____

BIRDS - Lyrics

Animals that people study quite a bit
    That are _____ and are also _____
        We do classify as _____
        Now, we'll share with you some words
    So some interesting facts you won't forget

Characteristics are a _____ , two _____ and _____
    Several kinds of _____ which do different things
        There are some that help them _____
        Others make them more _____
    Fuzzy, _____ feathers are insulating

_____ of birds are light because they are _____
    So it's easier to _____ , and don't you know
        Both to _____ them when they're _____
        And for oxygen supplying
    They have _____ _____ to help them on the go

Eggs let _____ pass right on through the _____
    Often laid inside a _____ constructed well
        The eggs the parents _____
        Hatch their young and may _____
    Following their _____ supply—there's more to tell

The class of birds has many orders and _____
    Which are divided into _____ and _____
        But _____ thousand different kinds
        Are too many for your minds
    So forget about more verses, if you please

Fill in the blanks, you may use a word more than once.

air sacs
beak
birds
bones
cool
down
families
feathers
fly
flying
food
genus
hollow
incubate
legs
migrate
nest
nine
oxygen
shell
species
streamlined
vertebrate
warmblooded
wings

BIRDS - Objective

True or false

1 - _____   Birds are coldblooded vertebrates.
2 - _____   Air sacs are hollow structures connected to the lungs.
3 - _____   Oxygen can pass through the shell of an egg.
4 - _____   Down feathers are used for flight.
5 - _____   Birds have hollow bones.

Matching

6 - Eggs _____   A. Sitting on eggs to keep them warm.
7 - Contour feathers _____   B. Make the bird more streamlined.
8 - Aves _____   C. Name of class of birds.
9 - Migrate _____   D. Movement to a new environment.
10 - Incubate _____   E. Contain living embryos.

11 - What are six characteristics of birds?

1- _____
2 - _____
3 - _____
4 - _____
5 - _____
6 - _____

12 - Why are down feathers often used in clothing?

_____
_____

13 - What are talons and what are they used for? What kind of bird has them?

_____
_____
_____

Match the examples with the type of bird.

14 - _____ Osprey   L = Land birds
15 - _____ Macaw   G = Game birds
16 - _____ Kiwi   W = Water birds
17 - _____ Woodpecker   O = Oceanic birds
18 - _____ Pheasant   T = Tropical birds
19 - _____ Passenger Pigeon   F = Flightless birds
20 - _____ Pelican   P = Birds of prey
21 - _____ Vulture   E = Extinct birds
22 - _____ Heron
23 - _____ Parakeet
24 - _____ Dodo
25 - _____ Penguin

BIRDS - Essay

1 - Why do birds incubate their eggs? _____
_____
_____
_____

2 - How do penguins, hawks and ostriches use their wings differently?
_____
_____
_____

3 - How is an egg similar to a seed?
_____
_____

4 - Why are eggs such a nutritious food?
_____
_____

5 - Why is a bat not considered a bird?
_____
_____

6 - What are two advantages of air sacs? _____
_____

7 - Label the air sac system, describing what body parts are included.

1._____

2._____

3._____

DIGGING DEEPER
What are the differences between an ornithologist, a bird watcher and a birder?
_____
_____
_____

ALGAE, FUNGI AND NONVASCULAR PLANTS - Lyrics

Algae and fungi, lichen, moss and liverworts
All are _____ and reproduce by _____
Algae is classified by _____ into _____ groups
They can be _____ , or brown, _____ , red, or _____

Fungi lack _____ , they get energy other ways
Most by _____ , or _____
If they live on dead things, they are known as _____
If they feed on living things, then they're _____

Mushrooms and toadstools, _____ and mildews, _____ and rots
Are many kinds of fungi: some are good, some not
Lichen's really two things, living _____
(Helping each other): _____ and fungi

Mosses and liverworts, found in _____ environments
Are simple, green, _____ _____ -producing plants

Fill in the blanks, you may use each word more than once.

algae	fermentation	green	molds	spore
chlorophyll	fire	lichen	nonvascular	spores
color	five	liverworts	parasites	symbiotically
decomposing	golden	moist	saprophytes	yeasts

ALGAE, FUNGI AND NONVASCULAR PLANTS - Objective

True or false

1 - _____ Fungi are true plants.
2 - _____ Parasites are organisms that feed on dead matter.
3 - _____ Algae has vascular tissue.
4 - _____ Nonvascular plants live in moist environments.
5 - _____ Large algae, such as seaweeds are now considered a
                  vascular plant.
6 - _____ Plants need chlorophyll to make their own food.

Matching

7 - Green algae   _____
8 - Brown algae   _____
9 - Fire algae   _____
10 - Red algae   _____
11 - Golden algae _____

A. Includes most seaweeds including the kelps.
B. Includes diatoms; microscopic free floating
   algae that have cell walls made of silica.
C. Includes those algae that produce red tide and
   bioluminescence.
D. Includes those algae that live in ponds, lakes and
   streams; they do especially well in warm water.
E. Includes other seaweeds which can grow in deeper
   water than others.

Vocabulary matching

12 - Symbiosis   _____
13 - Saprophytes   _____
14 - Fruiting body _____
15 - Mutualism   _____
16 - Hyphae   _____
17 - Decomposers   _____
18 - Parasites   _____
19 - Germination   _____
20 - Chlorophyll   _____

A. Pigment needed for photosynthesis.
B. Sprouting of a seed.
C. A word that means "together life."
D. Organisms that feed on living things.
E. Organisms which break down living or dead things.
F. Thread-like strands that develop from fungus spores
   after germination .
G. A symbiotic relationship in which neither organism
   is harmed and both benefit.
H. Organisms that feed on dead things.
I. Fungi develop these for spore production.

Short Answer

21 - Algae is classified by _____.
22 - Fire algae are known for producing _____ and _____.
23 - Fungi lack _____ , used by plants for producing food.
24 - Fungi reproduce by _____.
25 - Lichen is a symbiotic relationship between _____ and _____.

ALGAE, FUNGI AND NONVASCULAR PLANTS - Essay

1 - What is the difference between saprophytes and parasites? _____
_____
_____

2 - How is yeast used in bread making ?_____
_____
_____
_____
_____

3 - What is mutualism? Give an example._____
_____
_____

4 - Describe four reasons why fungi are important (or list uses). _____
_____
_____
_____

5 - How are fungi different from plants and how do they get their energy? _____
_____
_____
_____
_____

6 - Name five kinds (general groups, not specific species) of fungi.
    1. _____
    2. _____
    3. _____
    4. _____
    5. _____

7 - Name the three types of lichen.
    1. _____
    2. _____
    3. _____

8 - Why are lichen sometimes thought of as "pioneers"? _____
_____
_____

DIGGING DEEPER
What is the importance of algae in marine food chains? _____
_____
_____
_____
_____
_____

VASCULAR PLANTS - Lyrics

Xylem carries _____ and _____ toward the sky
_____ carries food on down and that's the reason why-
The most important cells are those producing both of them:
The cells of the _____
Chorus: Vascular... Oh vascular plants
                _____... Oh vascular plants
               Vascular...Oh vascular plants
               All have _____ tubes

_____ and also horsetails are both vascular indeed
They reproduce by means of _____ and rhizomes, not by _____
The spores come from the _____ underneath the _____ of ferns
Growing into a _____
Chorus

Gymnosperms have _____ seeds which you may see
On the cones of _____ most often in a tree
Fir, pine, _____, cedar, _____ , redwood and juniper
Stay green throughout the year
Chorus

Gymnosperms with naked seeds and angiosperms with fruits
_____ the water from the _____ and held in place by _____
Food is made in _____ and then the stems help to _____
That food throughout the plant which they support
Chorus

Flowers may have _____, petals, _____ , and stamen
Ripened ovaries are _____ with _____ inside of them
Seeds have coats and _____ that are indeed alive
With food to help them survive
Chorus

CO_2 and _____ with light and energy
Glucose is made by _____ and oxygen's set free
(Respiration is the opposite of this process)
It's called _____
Chorus

Plants need _____, light and _____ with proper _____
Space to grow, and minerals , they need them to mature
Tropisms are responses to _____ , I'm told
By _____ they're controlled
Chorus

Fill in the blanks, you may use each word more than once.

absorb	ferns	leaves	roots	spores	transporting
air	fronds	minerals	seed	spruce	tropisms
cambium	fruits	phloem	seeds	stimuli	unprotected
chlorophyll	hemlock	photosynthesis	sepals	support	vascular
conifers	hormones	pistils	soil	temperature	water
embryos	H_2O	prothallium	sorus	transport	

VASCULAR PLANTS - Objective

True or false

1 - _____ All conifers are evergreens.
2 - _____ Ferns and horsetails are vascular, spore-producing plants.
3 - _____ Gymnosperms have seeds protected within a ripened ovary.
4 - _____ During photosynthesis, light energy is changed to chemical energy.
5 - _____ All fruit develops from flowers.
6 - _____ Angiosperms are the largest subgroup of vascular plants.

Label the three kinds of vascular tissue:

7 - _____

8 - _____

9 - _____

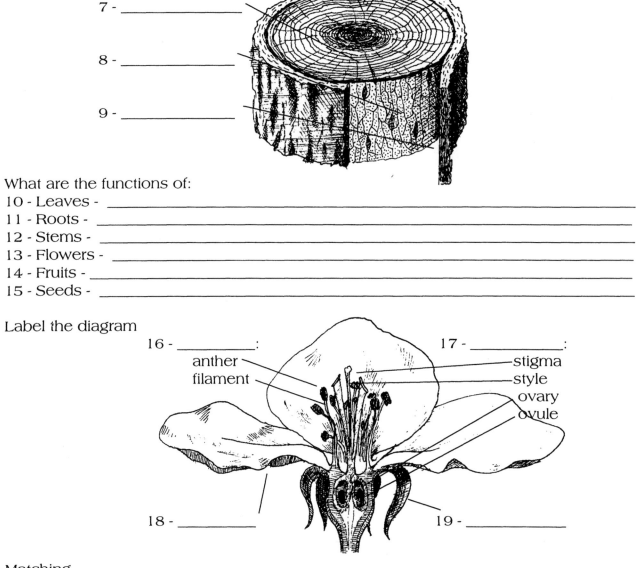

What are the functions of:

10 - Leaves - _____
11 - Roots - _____
12 - Stems - _____
13 - Flowers - _____
14 - Fruits - _____
15 - Seeds - _____

Label the diagram

16 - _____ :
anther
filament

17 - _____ :
stigma
style
ovary
ovule

18 - _____

19 - _____

Matching

20 - Geotropism _____   A. a process in which a plant makes its own food
21 - Phototropism _____   B. plants that drop their leaves in autumn
22 - Embryo _____   C. the sprouting of a seed
23 - Germination _____   D. growing toward light
24 - Photosynthesis _____   E. roots growing toward the pull of gravity
25 - Deciduous _____   F. A plant in its beginning stage

VASCULAR PLANTS - Essay

1 - What does girdling do to a tree?_____
_____

2 - How are gymnosperms and angiosperms different?_____
_____
_____
_____
_____

3 - Explain what makes plant roots and stems grow in different directions. _____
_____
_____
_____

4 - What is the difference between pollination, fertilization and germination?
_____
_____
_____

5 - Why don't all plants need soil? _____
_____
_____

DIGGING DEEPER

1 - Explain why deciduous trees drop their leaves in autumn. _____
_____
_____
_____

2 - How are plants used to classify regions such as different kinds of forests, deserts
and grasslands? _____
_____
_____
_____
_____
_____

PROTOZOA - Lyrics

How they _____ is how you know
Into which _____ they will go
Here are four groups with some _____
So you understand how they are_____

Chorus: Protozoa, also called _____:
       They're _____ and are single-celled
      _____, also called protista:
       They're microscopic and are _____

_____ are a sarcodine
_____ to move are seen
False feet arrange the _____ to change
And remember that the _____ are called:

Chorus

All around the _____
You can see some moving _____
Tiny _____ are wiggling there
And remember that the _____ are called:

Chorus

At the tail end of the _____
They will all have a _____
The _____ to whip is from the tip
And I know that the _____ are called:

Chorus

_____ live in a host
Movement's limited the most
_____ carried by a _____
The _____ is moved to a new _____

Chorus

Fill in the blanks, you may use words more than once.
amoebas
cilia
ciliates
classified
euglena
examples
false feet
flagella
flagellates
group
hairs
host
malaria's
microscopic
mosquito
move
paramecia
plasmodium
protista
protozoa
pseudopods
sarcodines
shape
single-celled
sporozoans
tail

PROTOZOA - Objective

True or false

1 - _____ Some protozoa are made up of many cells.
2 - _____ Plasmodium is a type of mosquito.
3 - _____ Flagella help propel amoebas.
4 - _____ Some protozoa have chlorophyll.
5 - _____ Malaria is a leading cause of death worldwide.
6 - _____ Pseudopods are "false feet" on sarcodines.
7 - _____ Amoebas digest food through a vacuole in their nucleus.
8 - _____ Amoebic dysentary is spread by mosquitoes.

Match the type of protozoa with an example

9 - Sarcodine   _____   A. Euglena
10 - Ciliate   _____   B. Amoeba
11 - Sporozoan   _____   C. Paramecia
12 - Flagellate   _____   D. Plasmodium

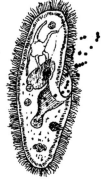

Match the protozoa with their characteristic for locomotion.

13 - Euglena   _____   A. Pseudopod
14 - Plasmodium   _____   B. Cilia
15 - Paramecia   _____   C. Flagella
16 - Amoeba   _____   D. host
17 - Volvox   _____

Short answer

18 - Protozoa are classified by the way they _____.
19 - Paramecia have _____to help them move.
20 - Protozoa most commonly reproduce by _____ _____.
21 - _____ is the name of a ball-like colony of many flagellates.
22 - _____ are the group of protozoans carried by their hosts.
23 - A particular species of _____ carries plasmodium.
24 - A _____ is a whip-like structure at one end of Euglena.
25 - Euglena can make their own food because they have _____.

PROTOZOA - Essay

1 - Describe the amoeba's eating habits. _____
_____
_____

2 - Describe how a ciliate eats. _____
_____
_____

3 - Describe how Euglena is unique in the way it gets energy. _____
_____
_____

4 - What protozoan is responsible for so many deaths worldwide? What is the
disease? How can the disease be controlled? _____
_____
_____
_____
_____

5 - Describe the life cycle of Plasmodium. _____
_____
_____
_____
_____

DIGGING DEEPER
Describe the importance of protozoa in a pond ecosystem._____
_____
_____
_____
_____
_____

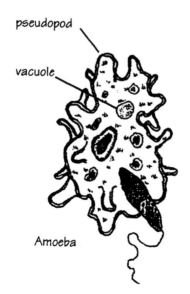

pseudopod

vacuole

Amoeba

GENETICS - Lyrics

_____ is what they say
    Made you what you are today
Like a _____ it will tell
    What will happen in each _____

DNA is a _____
    Look real close, it's really cool
Like a ladder in a _____ _____
    So simple yet so _____

Chorus: _____—
    Talkin' 'bout genes and _____
    De-oxy-ribo-nucleic acid—
    Talkin' 'bout _____ and chromosomes

In _____ made of DNA
    There is a particular way
_____ _____ can be seen
    In special orders to make a _____

When organisms _____
    Different _____ are on the loose
_____ and/or _____
    The offspring get _____ the parents give

Chorus

_____ is the study of _____,
    It may use _____
To _____ just how likely
    Results of genetic crosses will be

Chorus

Genetic _____ can use
    Parts of different _____
Changing _____ around
    To solve a _____ they have found

Chorus

Fill in the blanks, you may use words more than once.
cell
chromosomes
complex
deoxyribonucleic acid
DNA
dominant
double helix
engineers
gene
genes
genetics
heredity
molecule
molecules
nitrogen bases
orders
predict
probability
problem
program
recessive
reproduce
traits

26

GENETICS - Objective

True or false
1 - _____ Each person's DNA is unique.
2 - _____ Gregor Mendel is considered the father of biotechnology.
3 - _____ Gregor Mendel studied the characteristics of inheritance in peas.
4 - _____ A trait is determined by the DNA in the cells.
5 - _____ There are hundreds of different kinds of nitrogen bases.

Matching
 6 - Traits   _____   A. What chromosomes are made of.
 7 - Dominant   _____   B. Term to describe how likely something may happen.
 8 - Genes   _____   C. Thread-like structures of hereditary material.
 9 - Double helix   _____   D. Characteristics inherited from the parents.
10 - DNA   _____   E. Substances on the "rungs" of the double helix.
11 - Inherit   _____   F. Factors that determine the traits the offspring get.
12 - Recessive   _____   G. Passed down from the parent to the offspring.
13 - Chromosome   _____   H. Traits that show up more often.
14 - Probability   _____   I. The shape of the DNA molecule.
15 - Nitrogen bases   _____   J. Traits that do not show up often.

Fill in the blank
16 - Genetics is the study of _____.
17 - _____ or genetic engineering involves transferring parts of DNA molecules.
18 - _____ instructs and controls what happens in a cell.
19 - Genes are located on the _____.
20 - The "rungs" of DNA molecule are made up of different _____ _____.
21 - In 1953 two scientists were able to describe the chromosome as being a complex molecule called DNA, which stands for _____.
22 - A person's _____ is unique and can be useful in identifying specific individuals.
23 - The combination of two DNA molecules that have been spliced together is called _____ DNA.
24 - Traits which show up the most are called _____ traits.
25 - The factors that determine what traits the offspring get are called _____.

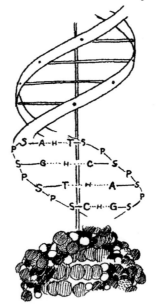

GENETICS - Essay

1 - Describe dominant and recessive genes, give examples of each. _____
_____
_____
_____

2 - How do you think the recording of data was important to Mendel's work with peas?
_____
_____
_____
_____

3 - How is an understanding of genetics important in breeding animals such as
horses, dogs and cattle?_____
_____
_____
_____
_____

4 - How is DNA like a computer program? _____
_____
_____

5 - Describe the relationships between DNA molecules, genes and chromosomes.
_____
_____
_____
_____

DIGGING DEEPER
1 - What would be an advantage of using DNA instead of fingerprints for solving
crimes? _____
_____
_____
_____

2 - Describe traits you have inherited from your parents and grandparents. _____
_____
_____
_____
_____

VIRUSES - Lyrics

Viruses cause many different _____ diseases
Influenza, common _____ (with fevers, coughs and sneezes)
_____ , _____ pneumonia, and mononucleosis
Chicken pox, _____ and mumps, _____ , _____

Chorus: Viruses are very _____
             Extremely _____
             Few of them are good at all
             From them the _____ may become sick

Viruses are _____ living, but are just tiny _____
Can't perform _____ functions; are _____ cells and don't contain _____
_____ only within a living cell and will take most
Of that cell's own _____ to multiply inside a _____

Chorus

In the _____ of viruses you'll find _____ acids
_____ which do control production of new _____
_____ or _____, under close inspection
Are surrounded by a _____ of _____ for _____

Chorus

Fill in the blanks, you may use each word more than once.				
AIDS	core	measles	particles	reproduce
cells	DNA	microscopic	processes	RNA
coat	host	molecules	protection	small
cold	infectious	not	protein	viral
conjunctivitis	life	nucleic	rabies	viruses

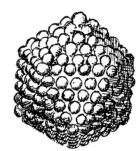

VIRUSES - Objective

True or false

1 - _____ A virus can carry on metabolic activities.
2 - _____ Nucleic acids are located in the core of viruses.
3 - _____ HIV is the most common virus.
4 - _____ Viruses are about the same size as most bacteria.
5 - _____ Viruses reproduce themselves using an organism's cells.

Matching

6 - Common Cold _____
7 - Rabies _____
8 - Mononucleosis _____
9 - Pneumonia _____
10 - Influenza _____
11 - HIV _____
12 - Conjunctivitis _____
13 - Polio _____
14 - Smallpox _____
15 - Yellow fever _____
16 - Hepatitis _____
17 - Tobacco Mosaic
       Virus _____

A. Several kinds of diseases that affect the liver.
B. Many Native Americans died from this disease brought to the Americas by European explorers.
C. The virus that causes AIDS.
D. Viral disease that means *rage* or *madness* in Latin.
E. Viral disease that caused a pandemic in 1918-1919 that killed 20 million people.
F. A lung disease caused by a virus or bacteria.
G. Viral disease that raises the number of white blood cells.
H. Most widely spread viral disease.
I. Disease caused by a virus carried by a mosquito.
J. A vaccine was developed in 1954 to prevent this crippling disease.
K. Virus that attacks tobacco and related plants.
L. Virus or bacteria that causes swelling of tissues around the eye.

Fill in the blank

18 - The core of a virus is surrounded by a coat of _____.
19 - A virus infects an organism through a particular cell called the _____ or host cell.
20 - A virus makes the living cell reproduce _____ cells instead of living cells.

Name three common childhood viral diseases now controlled by vaccines.

21 - _____
22 - _____
23 - _____

List the two basic parts of a virus.

24 - _____
25 - _____

VIRUSES - Essay

1 - Describe how viruses use living cells to reproduce themselves._____
_____
_____
_____
_____

2 - Infectious diseases are most commonly spread by:
    1. _____
    2. _____
    3. _____

3 - Discuss two reasons why the common cold is so difficult to treat.
    1. _____
       _____
    2. _____
       _____

4 - Why can a doctor prescribe antibiotics for a bacterial disease but not for a viral disease?_____
_____

5 - Why is HIV considered such a serious disease? _____
_____
_____
_____
_____

DIGGING DEEPER
Compare and contrast viruses which attack computers with viruses which attack living organisms. _____
_____
_____
_____
_____
_____
_____

OH BACTERIA - Lyrics

Oh lacking any_____, you do have a cell _____
You live in water, _____ and soil, and _____ at all
You reproduce by _____, and you do so _____ fast
And under harsh conditions in an _____ you last

   Chorus: Oh bacteria, though _____ and so small
          Without you _____ would not function well at all

For _____ things that die, a _____ we need
But some are _____, on a living host will feed
For taking _____ from air, and fixing it into
The soil for _____ to use, I'm sure they're all grateful to you

   Chorus: Oh bacteria, though simple and so _____
          Without you ecosystems would not function well at all

In _____ products you have shown yourself a _____ friend
And to genetic _____, your _____ you lend.
You even help to fight _____ caused by your brethren
You make _____ which destroy or _____ them

   Chorus: Oh, bacteria, though only _____
          A most important _____ we have now beheld

Though most of you are helpful, in some of these mentioned ways
There are a few who have to do, a bit with some _____
Producing _____ or the cells attacking _____
_____, pneumonia, strep throat, _____ , and _____

   Chorus: Oh bacteria, though only _____
          A most important _____ we have now beheld

We do appreciate you and your praises we do sing
Yet some of you make life so hard with _____ that you bring
Our food you _____, our crops you _____, our animals attack
With _____, different rots, cholera and _____

   Chorus: Oh bacteria, though only single-celled
          A most important organism we have now beheld

Fill in the blanks, you may use words more than once.

air
anywhere
anthrax
antibiotics
botulism
cultured
dairy
decomposing
diptheria
disease
diseases
DNA
ecosystems
endospore
engineers
fission
nitrogen
nucleus
organism
parasitic
plants
rot
saprophyte
simple
single-celled
small
spoil
TB
tetanus
toxins
troubles
very
wall
weaken

BACTERIA - Objective

True or False

1 - _____ Bacteria are many-celled organisms.
2 - _____ Bacteria do not have a nucleus.
3 - _____ Bacteria are important producers in ecosystems.
4 - _____ Bacteria are classified by shape.
5 - _____ Bacteria cells are similar to plant and fungi cells because they have a cell wall.

Match the scientists

6 - Anton Leeuwenhoek _____
7 - Robert Koch _____
8 - Louis Pasteur _____
9 - Joseph Lister _____

A. Discovered the cause of anthrax, cholera, and tuberculosis.
B. Used the germ theory to begin the use of antiseptic medicine.
C. Developed the use of vaccines and pasteurization.
D. Developed the first microscope.

Match the diseases

10 - Cholera _____
11 - Tuberculosis _____
12 - Anthrax _____
13 - Bubonic plague _____
14 - Diphtheria _____
15 - Tetanus _____
16 - Pneumonia _____
17 - Strep throat _____
18 - Pertussis _____
19 - Botulism _____
20 - Fire blight _____

A. Common contagious sickness that causes a severe sore throat.
B. Viral or bacterial disease that affects the lungs.
C. Disease that is carried by fleas on rats and killed one fourth of Europe's population long ago.
D. Also called "consumption."
E. A deadly disease of cattle and sheep.
F. Disease which causes the jaw muscles to become paralyzed. Bacteria enters the body through a cut or puncture wound.
G. A serious bacterial disease which attacks plants.
H. This bacteria can multiply inside an improperly sealed jar and cause a deadly food poisoning.
I. Whooping cough.
J. A very serious infectious intestinal disease spread by filthy conditions and poor sanitation.
K. Most often affects infants and is caused by a bacterium that lives in the nose and throat.

Fill in the blank

21 - Bacteria reproduce by _____ _____.
22 - _____ is the heating of liquids to kill bacteria.
23 - An organism that gets energy from decaying matter is called a _____.
24 - Bacteria often form _____ under unfavorable living conditions.
25 - An organism that feeds on a living host is called a _____.

BACTERIA - Essay

1 - Explain Pasteur's germ theory. _____
_____
_____
_____
_____

2 - Describe and give examples of the three shapes of bacteria. _____
_____
_____
_____
_____

3 - List four products developed to kill or weaken harmful bacteria and prevent
    infections.
    1. _____
    2. _____
    3. _____
    4. _____

4 - Describe four ways in which bacteria are considered helpful. _____
_____
_____
_____

5 - Describe how a vaccine works. _____
_____
_____
_____
_____

DIGGING DEEPER
Why were bacterial diseases more serious 150 years ago? _____
_____
_____
_____
_____

ANSWER KEY

P. 1 THE SCIENTIFIC METHOD

Oh, what do you think a <u>scientist</u> does
To solve a <u>problem</u> found because
Many <u>scientists</u> are scientists
Cause they're great <u>problem</u> solvers
There is a <u>systematic</u> way
They go about 'most every day
It's <u>methodical</u> and it's <u>logical</u>
The <u>scientific</u> method

Chorus: A way to <u>solve</u> a problem, a way, a way
The <u>scientific</u> <u>method</u> is a way to solve a <u>problem</u>
A way, a way, a way to <u>solve</u> a problem
A way, a way, a way to solve a <u>problem</u>

It may not seem important to you
But the <u>first</u> thing that they always do
Is state the <u>problem</u> or ask a <u>question</u>
So they know just what they're after
Then they <u>review</u> everything involved
That might help get the <u>problem</u> solved
By reading, <u>researching</u>
And gathering <u>information</u>
Chorus

After both of these <u>steps</u> they take
They go ahead and then they make
An educated guess—a <u>hypothesis</u> —
A possible <u>solution</u>
Then they use <u>scientific</u> tools
To <u>measure</u> and test some variable
In <u>experiments</u> which are really meant
To give more <u>information</u>
Chorus

This information they call <u>data</u>
They put together so that later
They can analyze and <u>synthesize</u>
To see just what it all means

Only when they have done all these
<u>Experiments</u> testing <u>hypotheses</u>
Which may prove, or else <u>disprove</u>
Then they'll state their <u>conclusion</u>
Chorus

This is the <u>systematic</u> way
A <u>scientist</u> may use any old day
'Cause it's <u>methodical</u> and it's logical
The <u>scientific</u> <u>method</u>

P. 2

1 - T	6 - E	11 - 5	17 - experiments
2 - F	7 - A	12 - 2	18 - possible solution
3 - F	8 - D	13 - 6	19 - data
4 - F	9 - B	14 - 1	20 - conclusion
5 - T	10 - C	15 - 4	
		16 - 3	

P. 3

1 - You have to know what is being looked for before starting to look for what is lost. In solving a math story problem, it is important to clearly know what is being asked. (This sounds so simple but is basic to the scientific method.)
2 - Gathering information is important because other people may have researched and experimented on the subject, and a scientist can then build on other's knowledge and progress further in his study.

For example, Pasteur built on the foundation of existing scientific information. Finding out what is known is more efficient than repeating what others have done.
3 - It is important to control variables so that one factor can be tested at a time. Pasteur controlled variables by using the same kind of swan-neck flask and the same exact procedure for collecting air. He also sealed the flasks before and after collecting air to prevent contamination.
4 - It would not be scientific, nor logical, nor even make sense to: state a conclusion before experimenting, to analyze data before collecting it, or try to solve a problem before knowing what the problem was.
5 - Data is often easier to analyze if it is in the form of a graph, table or chart.

DIGGING DEEPER
1 - After working hard to prove that a hypothesis was true, a scientist might not want to believe or accept data that would prove his hypothesis (and all his work) to be false. This was a problem that other scientists had with Louis Pasteur's germ theory. It took many years and repeated experiments to finally convince the other scientists to change their hypotheses. Knowing the truth may involve admitting being wrong, good scientists are willing to change what they believe when proved they are incorrect.
2 - Theory: A theory is the most logical explanation, based on available information.
   Law: a law is a theory that is generally accepted as true, having been tested many times, in many ways and by many people.

P. 4 ALL LIVING THINGS

All living things are able to <u>reproduce</u>
Move and <u>grow</u> and respond to a <u>stimulus</u>
And carry on <u>metabolic</u> activities
These are <u>characteristics</u> of living things

There are four metabolic <u>activities</u>:
Ingestion and <u>digestion</u> are two of these
<u>Respiration</u> and excretion
Metabolic, metabolic: <u>chemical</u> activities

Needs of living things include <u>energy</u>
Water, <u>oxygen</u> and food to eat
Living space and proper <u>temperatures</u>
All living things have these <u>six</u> basic needs

Living things are all made up of <u>cells</u>
Units of <u>structure</u> and functions you can tell
All <u>cells</u> come only from other living <u>cells</u>
This is what's called the <u>cell</u> theory

<u>Cells</u> that are similar joined together form <u>tissues</u>
<u>Tissues</u> working together form <u>organs</u>
Organ <u>systems</u> and <u>organisms</u> are:
Five levels in which living things are <u>organized</u>

Kingdom, <u>phylum</u>, class, <u>order</u>, <u>family</u>
Genus and <u>species</u> make the <u>name</u> you see
<u>Nomenclature</u> and taxonomy
Classify, classify, name and classify

P. 5

1 - C	6 - 2	11 - 2	18 - Genus
2 - E	7 - 1	12 - 4	19 - Species
3 - B	8 - 5	13 - 1	20 - energy
4 - D	9 - 3	14 - 5	21 - water
5 - A	10 - 4	15 - 7	22 - oxygen
		16 - 6	23 - food
		17 - 3	24 - living space
			25 - proper temperatures

Answer Key

P. 6

1 - 1. living things are all made up of cells
    2. cells are the basic units of structure and function
    3. all cells come from other living cells
2 - Producer: changes light energy form the sun
    to chemical energy (sugar or glucose)
    Example: any p(ant
3 - Primary consumer: eats plants
    Example: Rabbit or any herbivore
4 - Secondary consumer: eats primary consumer
    Example: Hawk or any carnivore
5 - Decomposer: breaks down living things after they die.
    Example: fungi or bacteria
6 - plant
7 - animal
8 - 1. presence of a cell wall
    2. presence of chlorophyll (chloroplasts)

DIGGING DEEPER
1 - Continent
2 - Country
3 - State
4 - County or parish
5 - City
6 - Street name
7 - Street number
8 - Scientific names are always the same, anywhere and in any language. Many organisms have more than one common name which may vary from place to place and in different languages.

P. 7 INVERTEBRATES

Many <u>creatures</u> have different features
    yet all have a common <u>trait</u>:
with no backbone they are all known
    to be called <u>invertebrate</u>

All invertebrates together make a bit
    over <u>eighty-nine</u> percent
Of the animal species in the world
    they live in any <u>habitat</u>

They're divided into <u>phyla</u>,
    by their <u>structures</u> classified
Here are eight kinds if you do find
    can then be identified

<u>Poriferans</u> are really sponges
    and they all have tiny <u>pores</u>
Cells in colonies they surely are pleased
    living on the ocean floor

Cnidarians like jellyfish, coral
    hydra, sea anemone
Cells for <u>stinging</u> have one opening
    <u>hollow</u> body cavity

Platyhelminths are the <u>flatworms</u>
    like the small planarians
Nematodes are little <u>roundworms</u>
    segmented worms are <u>annelids</u>

Echinoderms have <u>spiny</u> skins and
    tube feet coming out of them
Sea cucumber, <u>starfish</u>, sand dollar
    and the spiny sea urchin

Slugs and snails are one-shelled <u>mollusks</u>
    clams ans scallops have <u>two</u> shells
Octopus, squid, nautilus are
    headfooted with <u>tentacles</u>

They all have a softish body
    with a <u>mantle</u> that can make
A hard shell that you can tell will
    give <u>protection</u> for their sake

Arthropods have jointed legs
    and a hard <u>exoskeleton</u>
Centipedes, millipedes, insects
    arachnids, crustaceans

Centipedes have fewer legs and
    they are also <u>carnivores</u>
Millipedes have many more legs
    <u>scavengers</u> and herbivores

Crabs and lobsters, <u>shrimp</u> and barnacles
    are <u>crustaceans</u> you can tell
Four <u>antennae</u> legs are many
    they're aquatic with a shell

Arachnids include the spiders
    ticks and mites and <u>scorpions</u>
They all have <u>eight</u> legs two body parts
    no antennae and no wings

Insects have <u>six</u> legs, three body parts
    <u>two</u> antennae and two eyes
Egg to <u>larva</u> change to <u>pupa</u>
    then to <u>adult</u> with wings to fly

P. 8

1 - F	11 - F
2 - H	12 - G
3 - A	13 - C
4 - G	14 - A
5 - B	15 - B
6 - C	16 - D
7 - D	17 - E
8 - E	18 - C
9 - H	19 - B
10 - B	20 - A

P. 9

1 - Poriferans, Cnidarians, Echinoderms, Platyhelminths, Mollusks, Arthropods (crustaceans)
2 - Egg hatches into a caterpillar (larva) which changes into a pupa. The pupa is a resting stage which finally hatches out as an adult.
3 - Invertebrates are classified by their structures (body parts)
4 - Poriferans obtain their food from the water that passes through the pores. They are filter feeders.
5 - P, P, C, G, C, P, P
6 - The characteristics used to identify classes of arthropods are number of legs, number of body segments, plus features related to antennae, eyes, wings and mouth-parts.
7 - Flight gives insects advantages over other invertebrates by being able to find food, migrate to new habitats, escape form predators and easily find mates.

Digging Deeper
1 - Metamorphosis - different stages have different feeding habits; adaptable to many habitats; flight, small size, exoskeleton for protection.
2 - Ctenophora - tentacled and non-tentacled comb jellies
Nemertina - ribbon worms
Rotifera - rotifers
Nematomorpha - horsehair worms, freshwater and marine hair worms
Ectoprocta - freshwater and marine moss animals
Brachiopoda - hinged and non-hinged lampshells
Sipuncula - peanut worms

Echiura - spoon worms
Tardigrada - water bears
Penastoma - tongue worms
Onychophora - velvet worms
Pogonophora - beard worms
Chaetongnatha - arrow worms
Hemichordata - acorn worms

P. 10 COLDBLOODED VERTEBRATES

Oh, when you study animals, they're some of which you're told
Whose <u>blood</u> will always stay quite warm:
 but some whose blood is <u>cold</u>
They can <u>survive</u> within a range
Of temperature except a change
That's too <u>extreme</u> can be so dangerous for animals
For coldblooded <u>vertebrates</u>; coldblooded animals

They must respond by what they do and so they move around
To find the proper <u>temperature</u> in water or on ground
Fish, <u>reptiles</u>, <u>amphibians</u>,
Whose temperature of blood has been
Controlled from <u>outside</u> not within these kinds of animals
These coldblooded vertebrates; coldblooded animals

The fish have <u>gills</u> instead of <u>lungs</u> to get their oxygen
And most have air <u>bladders</u> and <u>fins</u> to help them float and <u>swim</u>
Some are <u>jawless</u>, like lampreys
With cartilage like sharks and rays
But most have bony <u>vertebrae</u>, they're bony animals
They're coldblooded vertebrates; coldblooded animals

Amphibians lead double lives, that's how they get their name
They start in water, then go on <u>land</u>, which they like just the same
<u>Toads</u> have dry and bumpy skin
<u>Frogs</u>' is wet and smooth as in
The salamanders and <u>newts</u>, their kin. They're all <u>amphibians</u>
They're coldblooded vertebrates; coldblooded animals

Snakes and lizards are <u>reptiles</u>, along with <u>tortoises</u>
Whose legs are made for <u>walking</u>, not for swimming like <u>turtles</u>
Crocodiles have teeth that <u>show</u>
An <u>alligator's</u> will always go
Inside its <u>mouth</u> that's how to know these different animals
These coldblooded vertebrates; coldblooded animals

These animals are different in the way they reproduce
The fish must <u>fertilize</u> their eggs <u>externally</u> and loose
Amphibians' <u>jelly eggs</u> are wet
Reptiles' are <u>leathery</u> and set
To hatch on <u>land</u> where they will get to become animals
These coldblooded animals; coldblooded animals

P. 11

1 - F	6 - F	11 - water aquatic plants, gills, tail
2 - T	7 - D	12 - dry, scaly
3 - T	8 - A	13 - swim, stop, turn
4 - F	9 - C	14 - back bones, scales, bladders
5 - T	10 - B	15 - coldblooded, backbone

15 - Toads have dry and bumpy skin, frogs have wet smooth skin
17 - The female deposits the eggs which are externally fertilized
 with milt (sperm) from the male.
18 - Amphibians lay eggs in water; eggs have jelly-like coating.
 Reptiles lay eggs on land; eggs are leather.
19 - These amphibians breathe through their skin; the oil from
 our skin clogs the pores in their skin and they may suffocate.
20 - Tadpole: Adult frog:
 1. eats water plants   1. eats insects and other invertebrates
 2. breathes through gills 2. breathes through lungs
 3. has a tail   3. has no tail

P. 12

1 - A coldblooded vertebrate such as a snake keeps its body temperature constant by its behavior; moving into the sun to get warmer or into the shade to get cooler.
2 - Amphibian eggs are laid in water. Tadpoles or polliwogs hatch from eggs, eat water plants and breathe through gills. Tadpoles gradually lose their tail and grow legs to become an adult. Adults can live in water or on land, breathe through gills and are carnivores.
3 - Jawless fish - suction-cup mouth instead of jaw, no scales, no fins or air bladders, cartilage instead of bones.
Cartilaginous fish - cartilage instead of bones, jaws, no scales, have rough skin, no air bladders
Bony fish - scales, air bladders, bones, vertebrae
4 - Fish - eggs are laid in water, then fertilized outside the female.
Amphibians - eggs are fertilized within the female, then laid in water, and surrounded by a jelly-like coating.
Reptiles - eggs are fertilized within the female, then laid on dry land.

DIGGING DEEPER
Snakes are coldblooded and need the heat energy from the sun to warm them enough to move and live. Reptiles are adapted to live where summers are warm; they hibernate in winder

P. 13 BIRDS

Animals that people study quite a bit
That are <u>warmblooded</u> and are also <u>vertebrate</u>
We do classify as <u>birds</u>
Now, we'll share with you some words
So some interesting facts you won't forget

Characteristics are a <u>beak</u>, two <u>legs</u> and <u>wings</u>
Several kinds of <u>feathers</u> which do different things
There are some that help them <u>fly</u>
Others make them more <u>streamlined</u>
Fuzzy, <u>down</u> feathers are insulating

<u>Bones</u> of birds are light because they are <u>hollow</u>
So it's easier to <u>fly</u>, and don't you know
Both to <u>cool</u> them when they're <u>flying</u>
And for oxygen supplying
They have <u>air sacs</u> to help them on the go

Eggs let <u>oxygen</u> pass right on through the <u>shell</u>
Often laid inside a <u>nest</u> constructed well
The eggs the parents <u>incubate</u>
Hatch their young and may <u>migrate</u>
Following their <u>food</u> supply—there's more to tell

The class of birds has many orders and <u>families</u>
Which are divided into <u>genus</u> and <u>species</u>
But <u>nine</u> thousand different kinds
Are too many for your minds
So forget about more verses, if you please

P. 14

1 - F	6 - E	11 - 1. warmblooded
2 - T	7 - B	2. backbone
3 - T	8 - C	3. beak
4 - F	9 - D	4. two legs
5 - T	10 - A	5. wings
		6. feathers

12 - Down feathers are used in clothing because they are lightweight and good insulators (keep body heat in).

Answer Key

13 - Talons are very sharp, strong claws on birds of prey used to grasp the animals they catch.

14 - P   20 - O
15 - T   21 - P
16 - F   22 - W
17 - L   23 - T
18 - G   24 - E
19 - E   25 - F

P. 15

1 - Birds incubate their eggs to keep them warm enough to hatch. Birds are warmblooded but their eggs cannot produce enough heat on their own.

2 - Penguins use their wings to swim.
Hawks use their wings to soar.
Ostriches use their wings very little; they run instead.

3 - Both an egg and a seed have an embryo, stored food, and a protective shell.

4 - Eggs have all the nutrients needed to keep an embryo growing and developing.

5 - A bat does not have a beak or feathers and does not lay eggs. Instead, bats have lungs, teeth, fir and give birth to live young; bats are flying mammals.

6 - 1. cool the bird
    2. provide more oxygen to the muscles when the bird is flying

7 - 1. wings
    2. chest
    3. abdomen

DIGGING DEEPER
Ornithologist - studies birds as a science.
Bird watcher - watches birds as a recreation and hobby.
Birder - observes, counts and keeps records of observations of many different kinds of birds.

P. 16 ALGAE, FUNGI AND NONVASCULAR PLANTS

Algae and fungi, lichen moss and liverworts
All are <u>nonvascular</u> and reproduce by spores
Algae is classified by <u>color</u> into <u>five</u> groups
They can be <u>green</u> or brown, <u>golden</u>, red or <u>fire</u>

Fungi lack <u>chlorophyll</u>, they get energy other ways
Most by <u>decomposing</u> or <u>fermentation</u>
If they live on dead things, they are known as <u>saprophytes</u>
If they feed on living things, then they're <u>parasites</u>

Mushrooms and toadstools, <u>molds</u> and mildews,
    <u>yeast</u> and rots
Are many kinds of fungi: some are good, some not
Lichen's really two things, living <u>symbiotically</u>
(Helping each other): <u>algae</u> and fungi

Mosses and liverworts, found in <u>moist</u> environments
Are simple, green, <u>nonvascular</u> <u>spore</u>-producing plants

P. 17

1 - F   7 - D   12 - C   17 - E
2 - F   8 - A   13 - H   18 - D
3 - F   9 - C   14 - I   19 - B
4 - T   10 - E   15 - G   20 - A
5 - F   11 - B   16 - F
6 - T

21 - color
22 - red tide, bioluminescence
23 - chlorophyll
24 - spores
25 - algae, fungi

P. 18

1 - Saprophytes get their energy from decomposing dead plants and animals. Parasites feed on living organisms; they may or may not cause harm to the host but they certainly never help it.

2 - Yeast is made active by putting it in warm water. It is then added to flour dough, where it multiplies rapidly. Carbon dioxide gas is produced from the respiration of the yeast and this gas produces bubbles. These gas bubbles cause the dough to rise. Once the dough has risen, it is cooked, killing the yeast.

3 - Mutualism is a symbiotic relationship in which two organisms live together to the benefit of both. Examples: Lichen (alga and fungus) or mycorrhiza (fungus and plant root).

4 - Fungi are important because they decompose things that die. (If they did not, there would be more dead plants and animal bodies.) Fungi are important for the destruction they cause to wood in buildings (dry rot and wet rot), and to crops and animals (parasitic fungi). Fungi spoil food (molds), but can also be eaten as food (mushrooms).

5 - Fungi cells do not have chlorophyll and therefore cannot produce their own food. Instead, they get their energy from breaking down living or dead organisms.

6 - 1. mushrooms and toadstools
    2. molds
    3. mildews
    4. yeasts
    5. rots

7 - 1. fruitcose
    2. folios
    3. crustose

8 - Lichens are able to live where other plants cannot, such as on bare rocks. They are able to establish themselves and eventually provide a habitat, food and even soil for other organisms.

DIGGING DEEPER
Algae that floats around in the ocean is called phytoplankton. These microscopic plants are the base of the food chain, providing zooplankton (floating microscopic animals) with energy. Larger animals feed on the zooplankton, and are themselves eaten by even larger animals.

P. 19 VASCULAR PLANTS

Xylem carries <u>minerals</u> and <u>water</u> toward the sky
<u>Phloem</u> carries food on down and that's the reason why-
The most important cells are those producing both of them:
The cells of the <u>cambium</u>

Chorus: Vascular... Oh vascular plants
        <u>Vascular</u>... Oh vascular plants
        Vascular... Oh vascular plants
        All have transporting tubes

<u>Ferns</u> and also horsetails are both vascular indeed
They reproduce by means of <u>spores</u> and rhizomes, not by
    <u>seed</u>
The spores come from the <u>sorus</u> underneath the <u>fronds</u> of
    ferns
Growing into a <u>prothallium</u>
Chorus

Gymnosperms have <u>unprotected</u> seeds which you may see
On the cones of <u>conifers</u> most often in a tree
Fir, pine, <u>hemlock</u>, cedar, <u>spruce</u>, redwood and juniper
Stay green throughout the year
Chorus

Gymnosperms with naked seeds and angiosperms with fruits
<u>Absorb</u> the water from the <u>soil</u> and held in place by <u>roots</u>
Food is made in <u>leaves</u> and then the stems help to transport
That food throughout the plant which they support

Chorus

Flowers may have <u>sepals</u>, petals, <u>pistils</u> and stamen
Ripened ovaries are <u>fruits</u> with <u>seeds</u> inside of them
Seeds have coats and <u>embryos</u> that are indeed alive
With food to help them survive
Chorus

CO_2 and <u>H_2O</u> with light and energy
Glucose is made by <u>chlorophyll</u> and oxygen's set free
(Respiration is the opposite of this process)
It's called <u>photosynthesis</u>
Chorus

Plants need <u>water</u>, light and <u>air</u> with proper <u>temperature</u>
Space to grow, and minerals, they need them to mature
Tropisms are responses to <u>stimuli</u>, I'm told
By <u>hormones</u> they're controlled
Chorus

P. 20

1 - T	10 - photosynthesis (food production)
2 - T	11 - absorb water and nutrients and hold
3 - F	the plant in place.
4 - T	12 - support leaves and flowers;
5 - T	conducts water, nutrients and food.
6 - T	13 - reproduction
7 - xylem	14 - protect, disperse, and nourish seeds
8 - cambium	15 - reproduction
9 - phloem	

16 - stamen	20 - E
17 - pistil	21 - D
18 - petals	22 - F
19 - sepals	23 - C
	24 - A
	25 - B

P. 21

1 - Girdling damages or kills the cambium and phloem layers of cells around a stem or tree trunk. Without cambium cells, no new phloem can be produced ant the plant will die.
2 - Gymnosperms have seeds that are unprotected and produce pollen on male cones. Angiosperms have seeds that are protected by fruit of some kind, and produce pollen on flowers.
3 - Plant growth is controlled by hormones which respond to stimuli. Roots grow down toward the stimulus of gravity (geotropism). Stems grow in the opposite direction as the roots until the stimulus of light causes them to grow or bend toward the source of light (phototropism).
4 - Pollination is the transferring of pollen from the male part of the flower to the female part (in angiosperms from the anther to the stigma). Fertilization is the uniting of sperm (from the pollen) with the eggs (the ovule). Germination is the sprouting of a seed.
5 - See p. 46 on the needs of plants; soil is not listed. Plants normally get the water and nutrients they need from soil; and are held in place by roots in soil. The soil itself is not needed if these needs are met in some other way. Growing crops without soil is called hydroponics.

DIGGING DEEPER

1 - The tree's needs are reduced by dropping their leaves before the cold winter months. Deciduous trees lose their leaves in autumn and become dormant (decrease metabolic activity) during winter months when temperatures are lower and there is less sunlight.
2 - Most plants grow best in particular climates (temperature and rainfall), and animals depend on plants directly or indirectly. Therefore, by describing a region by the plants that grow there, a general understanding of the ecosystem can be communicated as well.

P. 22 PROTOZOA

How they <u>move</u> is how you know
Into which <u>group</u> they will go
Here are four groups with some <u>examples</u>
So you understand how they are <u>classified</u>

Chorus: Protozoa, also called <u>protista</u>:
        They're <u>microscopic</u> and are single-celled
        <u>Protozoa</u>, also called protista:
        They're microscopic and are <u>single-celled</u>
<u>Amoebas</u> are a sarcodine
<u>Pseudopod</u> to move are seen
False feet arrange the <u>shape</u> to change
And remember that the <u>sarcodines</u> are called:
Chorus

All around the <u>paramecia</u>
You can see some moving <u>cilia</u>
Tiny <u>hairs</u> are wiggling there
And remember that the <u>ciliates</u> are called:
Chorus

At the tail end of the <u>Euglena</u>
They will all have a <u>flagella</u>
The <u>tail</u> to whip is from the tip
And I know that the <u>flagellates</u> are called:
Chorus

<u>Sporozoans</u> live in a host
Movements limited the most
<u>Malarias</u> carried by a <u>mosquito</u>
The <u>plasmodium</u> is moved to a new <u>host</u>
Chorus

P. 23

1 - F	5 - T
2 - F	6 - T
3 - F	7 - F
4 - T	8 - F

9 - B	13 - C	18 - move	22 - Sporozoans
10 - C	14 - D	19 - cilia	23 - mosquito
11 - D	15 - B	20 - binary fission	24 - flagellum
12 - A	16 - A	21 - Volvox	25 - chlorophyll
	17 - C		

P. 24

1 - An amoeba uses its pseudopod to move toward and surround its food. It engulfs it, then digests it in a food vacuole.
2 - A ciliate uses its cilia to move food particles toward the oral groove (the opening that takes in the food).
3 - Euglena can ingest food, or because it has chlorophyll, can make its own.
4 - The protozoan responsible for so many deaths worldwide is Plasmodium, and the disease is malaria. The disease is best controlled by killing the mosquito that carries the Plasmodium.
5 - The Plasmodium grows and multiplies in a person's red blood cells. It reproduces and spreads by producing spores which are picked up when a mosquito sucks blood form the host. The Plasmodium in the mosquito's saliva is transferred to a new host when the mosquito bites to get blood.
DIGGING DEEPER
Some protists such as Euglena, contain chlorophyll and are able to make their own food. In this way they are considered producers. Most protozoa are consumers, feeding on bacteria, algae or on other protists. Many invertebrates that feed on protozoa are in turn eaten by fish or other vertebrates.

P. 25 GENETICS

DNA is what they say
   Made you what you are today
Like a program it will tell
   What will happen in each cell

DNA is a molecule
   Look real close, it's really cool
Like a ladder in a double helix
   So simple yet so complex

Chorus: Deoxyribonucleic acid—
        Talkin' 'bout genes and chromosomes
        De-oxy-ribo-nucleic acid—
        Talkin' 'bout genes and chromosomes

In chromosomes made of DNA
   There is a particular way
Nitrogen bases can be seen
   In special orders to make a gene

When organisms reproduce
   Different genes are on the loose
Dominant and/or recessive
   The offspring get traits the parents give
Chorus

Genetics is the study of heredity,
   It may use probability
To predict just how likely
   Results of genetic crosses will be
Chorus

Genetic engineers can use
   Parts of different molecules
Changing DNA around
   To solve a problem they have found
Chorus

P. 26

1 - T	6 - D	11 - G
2 - F	7 - H	12 - J
3 - T	8 - F	13 - C
4 - T	9 - I	14 - B
5 - F	10 - A	15 - E

16 - heredity
17 - Biotechnology
18 - DNA
19 - chromosomes
20 - nitrogen bases
21 - deoxyribonucleic acid
22 - DNA
23 - recombinant
24 - dominant
25 - genes

P. 27

1 - Dominant genes control traits which show up often, such as dark skin, hair or eyes. Recessive genes control traits which do not show up as ofter, such as light skin, hair or eyes.
2 - Mendel's recording of data was very important for him to understand what was happening with his experiments. Accurate and detailed records helped him keep tract of the different traits passed on from parent pea plants to second, third and fourth generations.
3 - Domestic animals are bred for desired traits to be passed on and undesirable traits to be bred our.
4 - DNA instructs and controls what happens in cells; a computer program instructs and controls what happens in a computer.
5 - Chromosomes are made of DNA molecules. A part of a DNA molecule responsible for a certain trait is called a gene. A gene is a particular order of nitrogen bases on a section of the DNA molecule.

DIGGING DEEPER
1 - Fingerprints are often difficult to obtain and they are easily smudged. DNA "fingerprints" are considered to be a positive way of identifying individuals and can be obtained from blood or hair.
2 - Features such as hair color, skin color, body size and build; shape of mouth, nose, eyes, face and ears (especially ear lobes); ability to roll tongue.

P. 28 VIRUSES

Viruses cause many different infectious diseases Influenza, common cold (with fevers, coughs and sneezes) Rabies, viral pneumonia and mononucleosis
Chicken pox, measles and mumps, AIDS, conjunctivitis

Chorus: Viruses are very small
        Extremely microscopic
        Few of them are good at all
        From them the host may become sick

Viruses are not living, but are just tiny particles
Can't perform life functions; are not cells and don't contain cells
Reproduce only within a living cell and will take most
Of that cell's own processes to multiply inside a host
Chorus

In the core of viruses you'll find nucleic acids
Molecules which do control production of new viruses
RNA or DNA, under close inspection
Are surrounded by a coat of protein for protection
Chorus

P. 29

1 - F	6 - H	11 - C	18 - protein
2 - T	7 - D	12 - L	19 - target
3 - F	8 - G	13 - J	20 - virus
4 - F	9 - F	14 - B	21 - measles
5 - T	10 - E	15 - I	22 - mumps
		16 - A	23 - rubella
		17 - K	

24 - core of hereditary (or genetic) material; RNA or DNA
25 - coat of protein

P. 30

1 - A virus' nucleic acids take over the host cell's processes. The host cell then produces more viruses instead of reproducing itself.
2 - 1. particles in the air (as from coughing and sneezing)
     2. direct contact
     3. contaminated food or drink
3 - 1. The common cold is difficult to treat because there are over one hundred different kinds of viruses that affect our noses and throats!
     2. The viruses are not living and so cannot be killed by antibiotics.
4 - Doctors can prescribe antibiotics to kill bacteria because they are alive. Viruses cannot because they are not really alive.
5 - HIV is considered such a serious disease because it affects the immune system. The human body is not able to fight off other disease organisms once its immune system is infected with HIV. Also HIV changes so fast the immune system cannot keep up.

DIGGING DEEPER
A computer virus is a miniature computer program designed to infect other computer programs. Once in a computer, these programs give instructions to the other programs. The result can be as harmless as a simple message such as "Hello, I'm here!" or as destructive as erasing all the information in the computer's memory, both on the hard drive and floppy disk!

Computer viruses are man-made, which makes them different from naturally occurring viruses that attack living organisms. A program is information encoded on a computer disk, which is different from a virus particle composed of DNA or RNA molecules surrounded by a protein coat. Yet, there are many similarities between the two, which is why computer viruses were named after the disease-causing viruses.

Both replicate (copy) using an outside system; another computer program or a living cell. Both are infectious, spreading from one system to another, sometimes quite rapidly and often without detection.

Both types of viruses could be classified into different kinds based upon the degree of destructiveness or the mode of replication (how they copy themselves). There are computer viruses that are able to change to prevent being detected by a virus-check, just as there are disease viruses, such as HIV, that are difficult to control partly because of their ability to change.

Viruses that attack computers can cause severe and expensive disruptions in business, government and communications. Likewise, viruses that attack animals can cause severe, expensive and even deadly disruptions of life and health in an individual, family or community.

P. 31 OH BACTERIA

Oh, lacking any nucleus, you do have a cell wall
You live in water, air and soil, and anywhere at all
Your reproduce by fission, and you do so very fast
And under harsh conditions in an endospore you last

Chorus:
Oh bacteria, though simple and so small
Without you ecosystems would not function well at all

For decomposing things that die, a saprophyte we need
But some are parasitic, on a living host will feed
For taking nitrogen from air, and fixing it into
The soil for plants to use, I'm sure they're all grateful to you

Chorus:
Oh bacteria, though simple and so small
Without you ecosystems would not function well at all

In dairy products you have shown yourself a cultured friend
And to genetic engineers, your DNA you lend.
You even help to fight diseases caused by your brethren
You make antibiotics which destroy or weaken them

Chorus:
Oh bacteria, though only single-celled
A most important organism we have now beheld

Though most of you are helpful, in some of these mentioned way
There are a few who have to do, a bit with some disease
Producing toxins or the cells attacking directly
Diphtheria, pneumonia, strep throat, tetanus, and underline{TB}

Chorus:
Oh bacteria, though only single-celled
A most important organism we have now beheld

We do appreciate you and your praises we do sing
Yet some of you make life so hard with troubles that you bring
Our food you rot, our crops you rot, our animals attack
With botulism, different rots, cholera and anthrax

Chorus:
Oh bacteria, though only single-celled
A most important organism we have now beheld

P. 32

1 - F	6 - D	10 - J	15 - F
2 - T	7 - A	11 - D	16 - B
3 - F	8 - C	12 - E	17 - A
4 - T	9 - B	13 - C	18 - I
5 - T		14 - K	19 - H
			20 - G

21 - binary fission
22 - Pasteurization
23 - saprophyte or decomposer
24 - endospores
25 - parasite

P. 33
1 - Pasteur developed the theory that microscopic germs, mostly bacteria, were all around us. His theory was that these microbes were carried on the dust in the air and spread in that way as well as by direct contact with contaminated surfaces. He thought these germs were the cause of disease, decay and fermentation. He also thought they could be killed by heat and kept from spreading by washing the hands.
2 - Bacilli are rod-shaped. Spirilla are spiral or comma-shaped. Cocci are spherical. If the cocci are lined in chains, they are in the subgroup streptococci, and if they are in bunched like grapes, they are staphylococci.
3 - sterile bandages, disinfectants, antibiotics, antiseptic ointments, antibacterial soaps, mouthwashes (*Listerine* is named after Joseph Lister).
4 - Bacteria are considered helpful as decomposers, breaking down dead plants and animals and returning minerals to the soil. Particular bacteria take nitrogen from the air and "fix" it into the soil, making it usable to plants. There are particular bacteria that live in the intestines of animals, aiding digestion. Other bacteria are helpful in disposing of sewage, digesting oil spills, producing biodegradable plastics and controlling insect pests.
5 - Shots called inoculations are given to humans or animals which trigger the production of antibodies. These tiny particles are part of the immune system and are specific to the germs they attack. When the human or animal is later infected with these specific germs, it is able to fight off the infectious germ with the antibodies it has already produced.

DIGGING DEEPER
Bacterial diseases were more serious when we did not know what caused them. The work of Koch and Pasteur led to the understanding that many specific diseases were directly caused by particular bacteria. A further understanding of those bacteria helped in the development of diseases. Vaccines, pasteurization and sterilization led to Lister's development of antiseptic medicine, which greatly reduced the spread of infectious diseases.

For additional copies of Lyrical Life Science tape, text, workbook or notification of new releases contact:

Lyrical Learning
8008 Cardwell Hill Road
Corvallis, Oregon 97330
Telephone 541-754-3579